Warning Disclaimer

The information provided in this cookbook is for educational purposes only and is not intended to be a substitute for professional medical advice, diagnosis, or treatment. Always seek the advice of your physician or other qualified health provider with any questions you may have regarding a medical condition. Never disregard professional medical advice or delay in seeking it because of something you have read in this book.

The recipes and nutritional information provided in this book are based on general guidelines for managing diabetes and may not be suitable for everyone. Individual needs and responses may vary. It is important to consult with a registered dietitian, certified diabetes educator, or healthcare provider to create a meal plan that meets your specific health needs.

The author and publisher are not responsible for any adverse effects or consequences resulting from the use of any recipes, suggestions, or procedures described in this book. Use of the information in this book is at the reader's own risk.

THE
CARNIVORE
TRANSITION

DIET FOR BEGINNERS

TABLE OF CONTENT

PART I

ABOUT THIS BOOK

PART II

KETO CARNIVORE (3-4 WEEKS)

PART V

STRICT CARNIVORE (100% ANIMAL FOODS)

PART I

ABOUT THIS BOOK

WELCOME TO THE CARNIVORE DIET COOKBOOK FOR BEGINNERS

Welcome to **"The Carnivore Diet Cookbook for Beginners 2024"**, your comprehensive guide to embarking on a transformative dietary journey.

This cookbook is designed to support beginners who are curious about the carnivore diet and are looking for a structured approach to transition seamlessly. With the growing interest in the health benefits of a meat-centric diet, this book aims to demystify the process and provide practical, enjoyable steps towards adopting this lifestyle.

The **Carnivore Diet** is more than just a way of eating; it is a holistic approach to nutrition that prioritises simplicity, quality, and natural foods.

Throughout this book, you'll find detailed explanations, tips, and insights that will help you understand the philosophy behind the diet, as well as the science that supports its benefits. By following the structured plan laid out in these pages, you'll be able to transition at your own pace, ensuring a sustainable and rewarding experience.

Tailored specifically for United Kingdom, all measurements are provided in metric units to ensure ease and accuracy in your cooking. The recipes are crafted with local ingredients in mind, making it easier for you to source what you need and enjoy meals that are both familiar and new.

Whether you're starting or looking to refine your approach, this book is your ultimate companion on the carnivore diet journey.

EXPLANATION OF THE FOUR-STEP TRANSITION

Embarking on the carnivore diet can be a significant lifestyle change. This diet, which focuses exclusively on animal-based foods, can seem daunting at first. To make this transition as smooth and sustainable as possible, we've broken it down into four manageable steps. Each step is thoughtfully designed to gradually increase your consumption of animal-based foods, allowing your body to adjust while you learn to enjoy the simplicity and benefits of this diet.

The initial transition to the carnivore diet involves shifting from a diet that likely includes a variety of plant-based foods to one that relies heavily, if not entirely, on animal products. This change can affect your body in several ways, including your metabolism, digestion, and energy levels. To mitigate potential challenges and discomforts, the four-step transition plan provides a gradual increase in animal-based food intake. This approach helps your body adapt over time, minimising the shock to your system and making the overall experience more pleasant and manageable.

The structured approach of the four-step transition ensures that you can maintain a balanced and enjoyable diet throughout the transition period. By slowly phasing out plant-based foods and increasing your intake of animal products, you allow your body to adjust at a comfortable pace. This method also gives you the opportunity to explore and appreciate the variety of foods available within the carnivore diet, from different cuts of meat to various preparation methods.

KETO CARNIVORE (3-4 WEEKS)

The first step is the Keto Carnivore phase, which blends the principles of the ketogenic diet with the carnivore diet. During this 3-4 week period, you will gradually reduce your intake of carbohydrates and increase your consumption of fats and proteins from animal sources. This phase is designed to help your body adapt to using fat as its primary fuel source, a state known as ketosis. By easing into ketosis, you can minimise potential side effects such as the "keto flu" and ensure a more comfortable transition.

In this phase, you'll enjoy a variety of delicious recipes that include both animal-based foods and low-carb vegetables. This blend allows your body to gradually get used to the higher fat intake while still providing some of the fibre and nutrients from plant-based foods. The goal is to reduce carbohydrate cravings and stabilise your blood sugar levels, paving the way for the next phase.

ANIMAL-BASED CARNIVORE (80% ANIMAL FOODS)

In the Animal-Based Carnivore phase, you will consume approximately 80% of your calories from animal-based foods. This relaxed carnivore approach still allows for some plant-based items, making it easier to adapt while enjoying a variety of flavours and textures. This phase helps you further reduce your dependency on carbohydrates and introduces you to the benefits of a more animal-centric diet without feeling too restrictive.

During this phase, you'll explore a wider range of animal-based foods, including different cuts of meat, fish, eggs, and dairy products. You'll also learn how to incorporate minimal plant-based foods that complement your meals, such as herbs, spices, and low-carb vegetables. This step is crucial for helping you identify the animal-based foods that you enjoy the most and that make you feel your best.

CLASSIC CARNIVORE (98% ANIMAL FOODS)

The Classic Carnivore phase focuses almost entirely on animal-based foods, with minimal plant-based inclusions. This step brings you closer to a pure carnivore diet, allowing you to experience the full range of its benefits. You'll notice improvements in energy levels, mental clarity, and overall health as your body becomes more efficient at using fats for fuel.

In this phase, you'll delve deeper into the carnivore diet by experimenting with different cooking methods and recipes that highlight the natural flavours of high-quality meats. You'll also start to pay more attention to the sourcing of your ingredients, opting for grass-fed, organic, and sustainably raised options whenever possible. This phase is about refining your dietary habits and fully embracing the simplicity and satisfaction of the carnivore lifestyle.

STRICT CARNIVORE (100% ANIMAL FOODS)

The final step is the Strict Carnivore phase, where you commit fully to an animal-based diet with no exceptions. This means consuming 100% of your calories from animal foods such as meat, fish, eggs, and dairy. This phase is designed for those who want to experience the ultimate benefits of the carnivore diet, including optimal health, weight management, and mental clarity.

By this stage, you will have fully adapted to the carnivore lifestyle and can enjoy the simplicity it offers. You'll have developed a deep understanding of your body's nutritional needs and how to meet them through a diet composed entirely of animal-based foods. This phase is about achieving and maintaining peak health, with meals that are nutrient-dense, satisfying, and straightforward to prepare.

*This detailed section introduces you to the structure and purpose of "**The Carnivore Diet Cookbook for Beginners 2024.**" Each phase is carefully crafted to help you transition smoothly and successfully into a carnivore diet, making it accessible and enjoyable for everyone.*

PART II

KETO CARNIVORE
(3-4 WEEKS)

TRANSITIONING TO KETO CARNIVORE

The Keto Carnivore phase is the first step in your journey towards a full carnivore diet. This initial phase combines the principles of the ketogenic diet with those of the carnivore diet, allowing for a smoother transition by gradually reducing carbohydrate intake while increasing fats and proteins from animal sources. This phase typically lasts for 3-4 weeks, during which your body adapts to using fat as its primary fuel source instead of carbohydrates.

UNDERSTANDING KETO CARNIVORE

The Keto Carnivore approach integrates key elements of the ketogenic diet, which focuses on high-fat, moderate-protein, and low-carbohydrate intake, with the carnivore diet, which emphasises consuming only animal-based foods. By blending these two dietary strategies, the Keto Carnivore phase helps your body enter a state of ketosis—a metabolic state where fat, rather than carbohydrates, is used as the primary energy source.

During this phase, you will gradually eliminate most carbohydrates from your diet, including grains, legumes, fruits, and high-carb vegetables. Instead, you will focus on consuming animal-based foods that are rich in fats and proteins, such as meat, fish, eggs, and dairy. This gradual reduction in carbohydrates helps minimise potential side effects, such as the "keto flu," and makes the transition to a full carnivore diet more manageable.

To ensure a balanced intake of nutrients, it's important to include a variety of animal-based foods in your diet. Different cuts of meat, organ meats, fish, and eggs provide essential vitamins, minerals, and amino acids. Dairy products like cheese and butter can also be included to add variety and richness to your meals.

Benefits of Keto Carnivore:

• **Smooth Transition to Ketosis:** By gradually reducing carbohydrate intake, your body adapts to using fat as its primary fuel source, making the transition to ketosis smoother and more sustainable.

• **Increased Satiety:** High-fat and high-protein foods are more satiating, helping to reduce hunger and control appetite.

• **Stable Energy Levels:** Fat is a more stable energy source than carbohydrates, leading to fewer energy spikes and crashes throughout the day.

• **Mental Clarity:** Many people report improved focus and mental clarity when in ketosis, as the brain efficiently uses ketones for energy.

• **Weight Loss:** The Keto Carnivore phase can kickstart weight loss by promoting fat burning and reducing overall calorie intake.

Tips for Success:

1. Gradual Reduction of Carbs: Start by slowly reducing your intake of carbohydrates. Replace high-carb foods with low-carb vegetables initially, and then gradually eliminate them as you progress through the phase.

2. Increase Healthy Fats: Incorporate healthy fats into your diet to ensure you are consuming enough calories and staying satiated. Good sources of fats include fatty cuts of meat, fish, butter, ghee, and animal-based oils like lard and tallow.

3. Stay Hydrated: Proper hydration is crucial during the transition to ketosis. Drink plenty of water throughout the day to stay hydrated and help flush out toxins.

4. Electrolyte Balance: As your body adjusts to a lower carbohydrate intake, it may excrete more electrolytes. Ensure you are getting enough sodium, potassium, and magnesium to prevent symptoms like fatigue, muscle cramps, and headaches.

5. Listen to Your Body: Pay attention to how your body responds to the changes in your diet. Adjust your food intake based on your energy levels, hunger cues, and overall well-being.

6. Meal Planning: Plan your meals in advance to ensure you have a variety of foods and avoid boredom. Batch cooking and prepping ingredients can save time and make it easier to stick to your diet.

7. Support System: Engage with a supportive community, whether it's online forums, social media groups, or friends and family who understand your dietary goals. Sharing experiences and tips can provide motivation and encouragement.

BREAKFASTS

BACON AND EGGS

INGREDIENTS

---

4 SLICES OF BACON

4 LARGE EGGS

SALT AND PEPPER TO TASTE

1 TABLESPOON OF BUTTER

(OPTIONAL)

METHOD	TIME	SERVING	DIFFICULTY
FRYING	15 MIN	2	EASY

METHOD

Frying ensures that the bacon becomes crispy while the eggs can be cooked to your desired doneness.

CALORIES	FAT	SATURATES	PROTEIN	CARBS	SUGARS	SALT	FIBRE
350	28g	10g	25g	1g	0g	2g	0g

DIRECTIONS

STAGE I

1. Heat a frying pan over medium heat.

2. Add the bacon slices to the pan and cook until crispy, turning occasionally. This should take about 5-7 minutes.

3. Remove the bacon from the pan and place it on a paper towel to drain excess fat.

STAGE II

4. In the same pan, use the bacon fat to fry the eggs. If needed, add a tablespoon of butter to the pan.

5. Crack the eggs into the pan, season with salt and pepper, and cook to your desired doneness. For sunny side up, cook for about 3 minutes without flipping. For over easy, flip the eggs and cook for an additional 1-2 minutes.

6. Serve the eggs with the crispy bacon on the side.

For perfectly cooked eggs, keep the heat medium-low and avoid overcooking. The yolks should be runny if you prefer sunny side up or over easy.

THE
SEASONING

Season the eggs lightly with salt and pepper to enhance the natural flavours of the dish.

KETO CARNIVORE PANCAKES

INGREDIENTS

4 LARGE EGGS

100 G CREAM CHEESE

2 TABLESPOONS OF COCONUT FLOUR

1/2 TEASPOON OF BAKING POWDER

PINCH OF SALT

BUTTER OR COCONUT OIL FOR FRYING

METHOD
FRYING

TIME
20 MIN

SERVING
2

DIFFICULTY
MEDIUM

METHOD

Frying these pancakes in butter or coconut oil ensures a golden, crispy exterior and a fluffy interior.

CALORIES	FAT	SATURATES	PROTEIN	CARBS	SUGARS	SALT	FIBRE
320	27g	16g	16g	5g	3g	0.8g	2g

DIRECTIONS

STAGE I

1. In a bowl, whisk the eggs and cream cheese together until smooth.

2. Add the coconut flour, baking powder, and salt to the mixture, and whisk until well combined. Let the batter sit for a few minutes to thicken.

STAGE II

3. Heat a non-stick frying pan over medium heat and add a small amount of butter or coconut oil.

4. Pour small amounts of the batter into the pan to form pancakes. Cook for about 2-3 minutes on each side, until golden brown.

5. Serve the pancakes warm with a dollop of butter or a drizzle of sugar-free syrup, if desired.

These pancakes should be golden brown on the outside and fluffy on the inside. Ensure the pan is well-heated before adding the batter to achieve the best texture.

THE
SEASONING

Season with a pinch of salt to balance the sweetness of the pancakes.

SAUSAGE AND EGG MUFFINS

INGREDIENTS

8 LARGE EGGS

200 G SAUSAGE MEAT

SALT AND PEPPER TO TASTE

50 G GRATED CHEDDAR CHEESE
(OPTIONAL)

BUTTER FOR GREASING

 METHOD
BAKING

 TIME
25 MIN

 SERVING
4

 DIFFICULTY
EASY

METHOD

Baking these muffins allows the sausage to cook through while the eggs set perfectly.

CALORIES	FAT	SATURATES	PROTEIN	CARBS	SUGARS	SALT	FIBRE
250	20g	8g	18g	1g	0g	1.5g	0g

DIRECTIONS

STAGE I

1. Preheat the oven to 180°C (350°F) and grease a muffin tin with butter.

2. Divide the sausage meat into 8 portions and press each portion into the bottom of the muffin tin cups to form a base.

STAGE II

3. Crack an egg into each muffin cup on top of the sausage base. Season with salt and pepper.

4. Sprinkle grated cheddar cheese on top of each muffin cup, if desired.

5. Bake in the preheated oven for 15-20 minutes, or until the eggs are set and the sausage is cooked through.

6. Let the muffins cool slightly before removing from the tin. Serve warm.

These muffins should have a firm, golden-brown top with the egg fully set. They can be stored in the fridge for a quick, easy breakfast throughout the week.

24

THE
SEASONING

Season each muffin with a dash of salt and pepper to enhance the savoury flavours.

SCRAMBLED EGGS WITH CHEESE

INGREDIENTS

---

4 LARGE EGGS

50 G GRATED CHEDDAR CHEESE

2 TABLESPOONS OF BUTTER

SALT AND PEPPER TO TASTE

METHOD	TIME	SERVING	DIFFICULTY
FRYING	10 MIN	2	EASY

METHOD

Frying gently over medium heat ensures soft, creamy scrambled eggs.

CALORIES	FAT	SATURATES	PROTEIN	CARBS	SUGARS	SALT	FIBRE
300	26g	14g	20g	1g	0g	1g	0g

DIRECTIONS

STAGE I

1. Crack the eggs into a bowl and whisk until fully combined. Season with salt and pepper.

2. Heat a frying pan over medium heat and add the butter.

STAGE II

3. Once the butter has melted and starts to bubble, pour the eggs into the pan.

4. Cook, stirring continuously, until the eggs are softly scrambled.

5. Add the grated cheddar cheese and stir until the cheese is melted and the eggs are fully cooked.

6. Serve immediately.

For perfect scrambled eggs, cook over medium heat and stir continuously to ensure a soft, creamy texture. Avoid overcooking to keep the eggs moist and tender.

THE
SEASONING

Season generously with salt and pepper to enhance the cheesy richness of the dish.

LUNCH AND DINNER

GRILLED CHICKEN THIGHS

INGREDIENTS

---

8 CHICKEN THIGHS, BONE-IN AND
SKIN-ON
2 TABLESPOONS OLIVE OIL
1 TEASPOON PAPRIKA
1 TEASPOON GARLIC POWDER
SALT AND PEPPER TO TASTE

METHOD	TIME	SERVING	DIFFICULTY
GRILLING	30 MIN	4	EASY

METHOD
Grilling gives the chicken a smoky flavour and a crispy exterior.

CALORIES	FAT	SATURATES	PROTEIN	CARBS	SUGARS	SALT	FIBRE
400	30g	8g	35g	1g	0g	1g	0g

DIRECTIONS

STAGE I

1. Preheat the grill to medium-high heat.

2. In a bowl, mix olive oil, paprika, garlic powder, salt, and pepper. Rub the mixture over the chicken thighs.

STAGE II

3. Place the chicken thighs on the grill, skin side down. Grill for 10-12 minutes on each side, or until the internal temperature reaches 75°C (165°F) and the skin is crispy.

4. Let the chicken rest for a few minutes before serving.

The grilled chicken thighs should have a crispy skin and juicy, tender meat.

THE
SEASONING

Season generously with the spice mix to enhance the natural flavours.

BEEF AND AVOCADO SALAD

INGREDIENTS

300 G BEEF STEAK (SIRLOIN OR RIBEYE),
1 TABLESPOON OLIVE OIL, 1
AVOCADO, SLICED, 1 CUCUMBER,
SLICED, 1 CUP CHERRY TOMATOES,
HALVED, 1 RED ONION, THINLY SLICED,
SALT AND PEPPER TO TASTE, JUICE OF 1
LEMON, 2 TABLESPOONS EXTRA VIRGIN
OLIVE OIL

METHOD	TIME	SERVING	DIFFICULTY
GRILLING AND ASSEMBLING	25 MIN	2	EASY

METHOD
Grilling the beef and assembling with fresh vegetables and avocado.

CALORIES	FAT	SATURATES	PROTEIN	CARBS	SUGARS	SALT	FIBRE
450	35g	10g	30g	10g	5g	0.5g	6g

DIRECTIONS

STAGE I

1. Preheat the grill to medium-high heat.
2. Rub the beef steak with olive oil, salt, and pepper.

STAGE II

3. Grill the beef steak for 4-5 minutes on each side for medium-rare, or until it reaches your desired level of doneness. Let it rest for a few minutes, then slice thinly.
4. In a large bowl, combine the avocado, cucumber, cherry tomatoes, and red onion.
5. Add the sliced beef to the salad. Drizzle with lemon juice and extra virgin olive oil. Toss gently to combine.
6. Serve immediately.

This salad should be fresh and vibrant, with the creamy avocado balancing the robust flavour of the grilled beef.

THE
SEASONING

Season the beef well before grilling to enhance its taste.

LAMB CHOPS WITH HERBS

INGREDIENTS

8 LAMB CHOPS
2 TABLESPOONS OLIVE OIL
2 CLOVES GARLIC, MINCED
1 TABLESPOON FRESH ROSEMARY, CHOPPED
1 TABLESPOON FRESH THYME, CHOPPED
SALT AND PEPPER TO TASTE

METHOD	TIME	SERVING	DIFFICULTY
GRILLING	20 MIN	4	EASY

METHOD
Grilling the lamb chops enhances their natural flavour and adds a smoky touch.

CALORIES	FAT	SATURATES	PROTEIN	CARBS	SUGARS	SALT	FIBRE
350	28g	12g	22g	1g	0g	0.8g	0g

DIRECTIONS

STAGE I

1. Preheat the grill to medium-high heat.

2. In a small bowl, mix olive oil, garlic, rosemary, thyme, salt, and pepper. Rub the mixture over the lamb chops.

STAGE II

3. Place the lamb chops on the grill and cook for 4-5 minutes on each side for medium-rare, or until they reach your desired level of doneness.

4. Let the lamb chops rest for a few minutes before serving.

The lamb chops should be juicy and tender with a hint of smokiness from the grill.

THE
SEASONING

Season generously with herbs to enhance their natural flavour.

KETO CARNIVORE MEATBALLS

INGREDIENTS

500 G GROUND BEEF

1 EGG

50 G GRATED PARMESAN CHEESE

2 CLOVES GARLIC, MINCED

1 TEASPOON SALT

1/2 TEASPOON BLACK PEPPER

1 TEASPOON DRIED OREGANO

METHOD	TIME	SERVING	DIFFICULTY
BAKING	30 MIN	4	EASY

METHOD

Baking the meatballs ensures they cook evenly and retain their moisture.

CALORIES	FAT	SATURATES	PROTEIN	CARBS	SUGARS	SALT	FIBRE
350	25g	10g	30g	2g	0g	1g	0g

DIRECTIONS

STAGE I

1. Preheat the oven to 180°C (350°F).

2. In a large bowl, combine ground beef, egg, Parmesan cheese, garlic, salt, black pepper, and oregano. Mix until well combined.

STAGE II

3. Form the mixture into small meatballs and place them on a baking sheet lined with parchment paper.

4. Bake in the preheated oven for 20-25 minutes, or until the meatballs are cooked through.

5. Serve warm.

These meatballs should be tender and juicy with a rich, savoury flavour.

THE
SEASONING

Adjust seasoning to taste and ensure they are evenly sized for consistent cooking.

BUTTER-BASTED RIBEYE

INGREDIENTS

2 RIBEYE STEAKS (ABOUT 300 G EACH)

2 TABLESPOONS OLIVE OIL

4 TABLESPOONS BUTTER

2 CLOVES GARLIC, CRUSHED

2 SPRIGS THYME

SALT AND PEPPER TO TASTE

METHOD

PAN-SEARING

TIME

20 MIN

SERVING

2

DIFFICULTY

MEDIUM

METHOD

Pan-searing and basting the ribeye with butter ensures a rich, caramelised crust and a juicy interior.

CALORIES	FAT	SATURATES	PROTEIN	CARBS	SUGARS	SALT	FIBRE
700	60g	25g	40g	1g	0g	1.2g	0g

DIRECTIONS

STAGE I

1. Heat a heavy skillet over high heat and add the olive oil.

2. Season the ribeye steaks generously with salt and pepper.

STAGE II

3. Place the steaks in the skillet and sear for 3-4 minutes on each side for medium-rare, or until they reach your desired level of doneness.

4. Reduce the heat to medium and add the butter, garlic, and thyme to the pan. Tilt the pan and spoon the melted butter over the steaks continuously for 1-2 minutes.

5. Remove the steaks from the skillet and let them rest for a few minutes before serving.

The ribeye should have a rich, caramelised crust and a juicy, tender interior. Basting with butter adds an extra layer of flavour and richness.

THE
SEASONING

Season generously for the best taste.

PART III

ANIMAL-BASED CARNIVORE (80% ANIMAL FOODS)

MOVING TO ANIMAL-BASED CARNIVORE

Transitioning to the Animal-Based Carnivore phase involves increasing your intake of animal-based foods to approximately 80% of your diet. This relaxed carnivore approach still allows for some plant-based items, making it easier to adapt while enjoying a variety of flavours and textures.

UNDERSTANDING THE RELAXED CARNIVORE DIET

The Animal-Based Carnivore phase, also known as the relaxed carnivore diet, balances a high intake of animal-based foods with a small percentage of plant-based items. This phase helps you gradually reduce your dependency on carbohydrates and introduces you to the benefits of a more animal-centric diet without feeling too restrictive. By allowing some plant-based foods, you can enjoy a wider variety of flavours and textures, making it easier to stick to the diet while still moving towards a more carnivorous approach.

BENEFITS OF ANIMAL-BASED CARNIVORE

- **Greater Variety of Flavours:** Including some plant-based foods can make meals more enjoyable and diverse.
- **Ease of Transition:** Gradually reducing plant-based foods makes the transition smoother and less abrupt.
- **Balanced Nutrition:** Combining animal-based foods with minimal plant-based items can help maintain balanced nutrition and prevent potential deficiencies.

Tips for Success:

1. **Focus on High-Quality Animal Foods:** Prioritise grass-fed, pasture-raised, and wild-caught animal products for maximum nutritional benefits.
2. **Incorporate Minimal Plant-Based Foods:** Use plant-based items sparingly to complement your meals and add variety without overwhelming the animal-based focus.
3. **Experiment with Different Meats and Fish:** Try various cuts of meat, organ meats, and different types of fish to keep your meals interesting and nutrient-dense.
4. **Monitor Your Body's Response:** Pay attention to how your body reacts to the changes in your diet and adjust accordingly to ensure you feel your best.
5. **Stay Hydrated:** Drink plenty of water and ensure adequate electrolyte intake to support your body's adaptation to the diet.
6. **Prepare and Plan Meals:** Plan your meals ahead of time to ensure you have a variety of options and avoid falling back on old eating habits.

BREAKFASTS

SCRAMBLED EGGS WITH SALMON

INGREDIENTS

4 LARGE EGGS

100 G SMOKED SALMON, CHOPPED

2 TABLESPOONS OF BUTTER

SALT AND PEPPER TO TASTE

METHOD	TIME	SERVING	DIFFICULTY
FRYING	15 MIN	2	EASY

METHOD

Frying ensures the eggs are fluffy and the salmon is lightly cooked.

CALORIES	FAT	SATURATES	PROTEIN	CARBS	SUGARS	SALT	FIBRE
300	24g	12g	22g	1g	0g	1.5g	0g

DIRECTIONS

STAGE I

1. Crack the eggs into a bowl and whisk until fully combined. Season with salt and pepper.

2. Heat a frying pan over medium heat and add the butter.

STAGE II

3. Once the butter has melted, pour the eggs into the pan.

4. Cook, stirring continuously, until the eggs are softly scrambled.

5. Add the chopped smoked salmon and stir gently until evenly distributed and heated through.

6. Serve immediately.

For perfectly scrambled eggs, cook over medium heat and stir continuously to ensure a soft, creamy texture.

THE
SEASONING

Season lightly to enhance the delicate flavour of the salmon.

YOGURT WITH BERRIES

INGREDIENTS

200 G FULL-FAT GREEK YOGURT

50 G MIXED BERRIES (BLUEBERRIES, RASPBERRIES, STRAWBERRIES)

1 TABLESPOON OF HONEY (OPTIONAL)

1 TEASPOON OF CHIA SEEDS (OPTIONAL)

TIME	SERVING	DIFFICULTY
5 MIN	1	EASY

CALORIES	FAT	SATURATES	PROTEIN	CARBS	SUGARS	SALT	FIBRE
250	10g	6g	15g	20g	15g	0.2g	4g

DIRECTIONS

STAGE I

1. Spoon the Greek yogurt into a bowl.
2. Wash and prepare the berries.

STAGE II

3. Top the yogurt with the mixed berries.
4. Drizzle with honey and sprinkle with chia seeds, if desired.
5. Serve immediately.

Choose a variety of fresh, seasonal berries to add natural sweetness and vibrant colours to your breakfast.

THE
SEASONING

Adjust the amount of honey based on your taste preference.

CARNIVORE OMELETTE

INGREDIENTS

4 LARGE EGGS

100 G COOKED BACON, CHOPPED

100 G SHREDDED CHEESE (CHEDDAR, MOZZARELLA, OR YOUR CHOICE)

2 TABLESPOONS OF BUTTER

SALT AND PEPPER TO TASTE

METHOD	**TIME**	**SERVING**	**DIFFICULTY**
FRYING	15 MIN	2	EASY

METHOD

Frying the omelette ensures it is cooked evenly and retains a soft, fluffy texture.

CALORIES	FAT	SATURATES	PROTEIN	CARBS	SUGARS	SALT	FIBRE
350	28g	14g	24g	2g	1g	1.5g	0g

DIRECTIONS

STAGE I

1. Crack the eggs into a bowl and whisk until fully combined. Season with salt and pepper.
2. Heat a frying pan over medium heat and add the butter.

STAGE II

3. Pour the eggs into the pan and cook until they start to set.
4. Add the chopped bacon and shredded cheese evenly over one half of the omelette.
5. Fold the other half of the omelette over the filling and cook until the cheese is melted and the eggs are fully set.
6. Serve immediately.

For a perfectly cooked omelette, ensure the pan is hot before adding the eggs and cook over medium heat to avoid browning.

THE
SEASONING

The filling should be warm and the cheese fully melted.

BEEF AND EGG MUFFINS

INGREDIENTS

200 G GROUND BEEF

8 LARGE EGGS

SALT AND PEPPER TO TASTE

BUTTER FOR GREASING

METHOD
BAKING

TIME
25 MIN

SERVING
4

DIFFICULTY
EASY

METHOD

Baking these muffins allows the beef and eggs to cook through evenly, creating a convenient, protein-packed breakfast.

CALORIES	FAT	SATURATES	PROTEIN	CARBS	SUGARS	SALT	FIBRE
300	22g	8g	24g	1g	0g	1.5g	0g

DIRECTIONS

STAGE I

1. Preheat the oven to 180°C (350°F) and grease a muffin tin with butter.

2. Divide the ground beef into 8 portions and press each portion into the bottom of the muffin tin cups to form a base.

STAGE II

3. Crack an egg into each muffin cup on top of the beef base. Season with salt and pepper.

4. Bake in the preheated oven for 15-20 minutes, or until the eggs are set and the beef is cooked through.

5. Let the muffins cool slightly before removing from the tin. Serve warm.

These muffins should have a firm, golden-brown top with the egg fully set. They can be stored in the fridge for a quick, easy breakfast throughout the week.

THE
SEASONING

Season each muffin with a dash of salt and pepper to enhance the savoury flavours.

LUNCH AND DINNER

ROAST CHICKEN

INGREDIENTS

1 WHOLE CHICKEN (ABOUT 1.5 KG)
2 TABLESPOONS OLIVE OIL
1 LEMON, HALVED
4 CLOVES GARLIC, CRUSHED
2 SPRIGS ROSEMARY
SALT AND PEPPER TO TASTE

METHOD	TIME	SERVING	DIFFICULTY
ROASTING	1 HOUR 30 MIN	4	MEDIUM

METHOD
Roasting ensures the chicken is cooked evenly with a crispy skin.

CALORIES	FAT	SATURATES	PROTEIN	CARBS	SUGARS	SALT	FIBRE
450	30g	8g	40g	2g	0g	1g	0g

DIRECTIONS

STAGE I

1. Preheat the oven to 200°C (400°F).

2. Rub the chicken with olive oil and season with salt and pepper.

3. Place the lemon halves, garlic, and rosemary inside the chicken cavity.

STAGE II

4. Place the chicken in a roasting pan and roast in the preheated oven for 1 hour 20 minutes, or until the internal temperature reaches 75°C (165°F) and the skin is golden and crispy.

5. Let the chicken rest for 10 minutes before carving.

6. Serve with the pan juices.

The roast chicken should have a golden, crispy skin with juicy, tender meat. Letting the chicken rest before carving ensures the juices redistribute for a moist result.

THE
SEASONING

Adjust seasoning to taste.

SHRIMP SKEWERS

INGREDIENTS

500 G LARGE SHRIMP, PEELED AND
DEVEINED, 2 TABLESPOONS OLIVE OIL
3 CLOVES GARLIC, MINCED
1 LEMON (JUICED) 1 TEASPOON
PAPRIKA
SALT AND PEPPER TO TASTE, SKEWERS

METHOD	TIME	SERVING	DIFFICULTY
GRILLING	20 MIN	5	EASY

METHOD

Grilling the shrimp on skewers ensures they cook evenly and quickly.

CALORIES	FAT	SATURATES	PROTEIN	CARBS	SUGARS	SALT	FIBRE
150	7g	1g	20g	1g	0g	0.8g	0g

DIRECTIONS

STAGE I

1. In a bowl, combine olive oil, garlic, lemon juice, paprika, salt, and pepper. Add the shrimps and toss to coat.

2. Preheat the grill to medium-high heat.

STAGE II

3. Thread the shrimps onto the skewers.

4. Grill the shrimp for 2-3 minutes on each side, or until they are pink and opaque.

5. Serve immediately with lemon wedges.

The shrimp should be pink and opaque when cooked. Ensure the grill is hot before cooking to get a nice char on the shrimp.

THE
SEASONING

Season generously to enhance the flavours.

BAKED COD WITH HERBS

INGREDIENTS

———

4 COD FILLETS (ABOUT 150 G EACH)

2 TABLESPOONS OLIVE OIL, 2 CLOVES

GARLIC, MINCED, 1 TABLESPOON FRESH

PARSLEY, CHOPPED, 1 TABLESPOON

FRESH DILL, CHOPPED

1 LEMON, SLICED

SALT AND PEPPER TO TASTE

METHOD	TIME	SERVING	DIFFICULTY
BAKING	25 MIN	4	EASY

METHOD

Baking the cod with herbs ensures a tender and flavourful fish.

CALORIES	FAT	SATURATES	PROTEIN	CARBS	SUGARS	SALT	FIBRE
200	10g	2g	25g	1g	0g	0.5g	0g

DIRECTIONS

———

STAGE I

1. Preheat the oven to 180°C (350°F).

2. Place the cod fillets on a baking sheet lined with parchment paper. Drizzle with olive oil and season with garlic, parsley, dill, salt, and pepper.

STAGE II

3. Place lemon slices on top of the fillets.

4. Bake in the preheated oven for 15-20 minutes, or until the fish is opaque and flakes easily with a fork.

5. Serve immediately.

The cod should be tender and flaky. Ensure it is cooked through but not overcooked.

THE
SEASONING

The fresh herbs and lemon add a bright, zesty flavour.

VENISON STEW

INGREDIENTS

500 G VENISON, CUBED, 2 TABLESPOONS OLIVE OIL, 1 ONION, CHOPPED, 2 CARROTS, CHOPPED, 2 CELERY STALKS, CHOPPED, 3 CLOVES GARLIC, MINCED, 1 CUP RED WINE (OPTIONAL), 4 CUPS BEEF BROTH, 2 BAY LEAVES, 1 TEASPOON THYME, SALT AND PEPPER TO TASTE

METHOD	TIME	SERVING	DIFFICULTY
SIMMERING	2 HOURS	4	MEDIUM

METHOD

Simmering the venison ensures a tender, flavourful stew.

CALORIES	FAT	SATURATES	PROTEIN	CARBS	SUGARS	SALT	FIBRE
300	15g	5g	30g	5g	2g	1g	2g

DIRECTIONS

STAGE I

1. Heat olive oil in a large pot over medium heat. Add venison and cook until browned on all sides.

2. Add onion, carrots, celery, and garlic. Cook until vegetables are softened.

STAGE II

3. Pour in red wine (if using) and beef broth. Add bay leaves, thyme, salt, and pepper.

4. Bring to a boil, then reduce heat and simmer for 1.5 to 2 hours, or until the venison is tender.

5. Serve hot.

The venison stew should be rich and hearty. Simmering the stew for a long time ensures the meat becomes tender and the flavours meld together beautifully.

THE
SEASONING

Season to taste.

PORK RIBS

INGREDIENTS

1 RACK OF PORK RIBS (ABOUT 1.5 KG)

2 TABLESPOONS OLIVE OIL

2 CLOVES GARLIC, MINCED

1 TEASPOON PAPRIKA

1 TEASPOON CUMIN

1 TEASPOON BLACK PEPPER

SALT TO TASTE

METHOD	TIME	SERVING	DIFFICULTY
BAKING	2 HOURS	4	MEDIUM

METHOD

Baking the ribs low and slow ensures they are tender and fall-off-the-bone.

CALORIES	FAT	SATURATES	PROTEIN	CARBS	SUGARS	SALT	FIBRE
600	45g	15g	40g	1g	0g	1.5g	0g

DIRECTIONS

STAGE I

1. Preheat the oven to 150°C (300°F).

2. In a bowl, mix olive oil, garlic, paprika, cumin, black pepper, and salt. Rub the mixture all over the ribs.

STAGE II

3. Place the ribs on a baking sheet lined with aluminium foil. Cover tightly with another sheet of foil.

4. Bake in the preheated oven for 2 hours, or until the ribs are tender and the meat is pulling away from the bone.

5. Serve immediately.

The pork ribs should be tender and juicy with a slightly crispy exterior. Baking them low and slow ensures the best texture.

THE
SEASONING

Adjust seasoning to taste.

PART IV

CLASSIC CARNIVORE (98% ANIMAL FOODS)

TRANSITIONING TO CLASSIC CARNIVORE

Transitioning to the Classic Carnivore phase involves increasing your intake of animal-based foods to approximately 98% of your diet. This phase focuses almost entirely on animal-based foods, with minimal plant-based inclusions, allowing you to experience the full range of benefits associated with the carnivore diet.

UNDERSTANDING THE CLASSIC CARNIVORE DIET

The Classic Carnivore diet is a more refined version of the carnivore lifestyle, emphasising the consumption of animal-based foods with very few, if any, plant-based items. This phase helps you to fully embrace the carnivore diet, focusing on high-quality proteins and fats from animal sources. By eliminating almost all plant-based foods, you can better understand how your body responds to a predominantly animal-based diet, improving your health and well-being.

BENEFITS OF CLASSIC CARNIVORE

• **Enhanced Nutrient Absorption:** Animal-based foods provide highly bioavailable nutrients, making it easier for your body to absorb and utilise them.

• **Improved Health Markers:** Many individuals report improvements in blood sugar levels, cholesterol, and other health markers.

• **Simplicity and Satisfaction:** A diet focused on animal-based foods can simplify meal planning and provide a high level of satiety.

Tips for Success:

1. **Prioritise Variety:** Include different types of meats, fish, and organ meats to ensure a broad range of nutrients.

2. **Choose Quality:** Opt for grass-fed, pasture-raised, and wild-caught animal products for the best nutritional profile.

3. **Monitor Your Body's Response:** Pay attention to how your body feels and adjust your food choices accordingly.

4. **Stay Hydrated:** Drink plenty of water and ensure you are consuming enough electrolytes to support your body's needs.

5. **Embrace Simplicity:** Enjoy the simplicity of meal planning and preparation that comes with a meat-based diet.

BREAKFASTS

STEAK AND EGGS

INGREDIENTS

2 RIBEYE STEAKS (ABOUT 200 G EACH)

4 LARGE EGGS

2 TABLESPOONS BUTTER

SALT AND PEPPER TO TASTE

METHOD

FRYING

TIME

20 MIN

SERVING

2

DIFFICULTY

EASY

METHOD

Frying ensures the steak is seared to perfection and the eggs are cooked to your preference.

CALORIES	FAT	SATURATES	PROTEIN	CARBS	SUGARS	SALT	FIBRE
600	45g	20g	50g	1g	0g	1g	0g

DIRECTIONS

STAGE I

1. Heat a heavy skillet over high heat and add 1 tablespoon of butter.

2. Season the steaks generously with salt and pepper.

STAGE II

3. Place the steaks in the skillet and sear for 3-4 minutes on each side for medium-rare, or until they reach your desired level of doneness. Remove the steaks from the skillet and let them rest.

4. In the same skillet, add the remaining tablespoon of butter and crack the eggs into the skillet. Cook to your preferred doneness.

5. Serve the steaks with the eggs on the side.

The steaks should have a rich, caramelised crust with a juicy, tender interior.

THE
SEASONING

Season the eggs lightly to complement the steak.

LIVER AND ONIONS

INGREDIENTS

400 G BEEF LIVER, SLICED

1 LARGE ONION, THINLY SLICED

2 TABLESPOONS BUTTER

SALT AND PEPPER TO TASTE

 METHOD
FRYING

 TIME
25 MIN

 SERVING
2

 DIFFICULTY
MEDIUM

METHOD
Frying ensures the liver is tender and the onions are caramelised.

CALORIES	FAT	SATURATES	PROTEIN	CARBS	SUGARS	SALT	FIBRE
300	15g	7g	30g	10g	5g	1g	2g

DIRECTIONS

STAGE I

1. Heat 1 tablespoon of butter in a skillet over medium heat.

2. Add the sliced onions and cook until caramelised, about 10-15 minutes. Remove from the skillet and set aside.

STAGE II

3. Add the remaining tablespoon of butter to the skillet. Season the liver slices with salt and pepper.

4. Fry the liver for 3-4 minutes on each side, or until cooked through but still tender.

5. Serve the liver topped with the caramelised onions.

The liver should be cooked just until tender, avoiding overcooking to prevent it from becoming tough.

THE
SEASONING

The caramelised onions add a sweet, rich flavour that complements the liver.

CARNIVORE BREAKFAST CASSEROLE

INGREDIENTS

8 LARGE EGGS

200 G GROUND BEEF

100 G BACON, CHOPPED

100 G CHEESE, SHREDDED (OPTIONAL)

SALT AND PEPPER TO TASTE

METHOD	TIME	SERVING	DIFFICULTY
BAKING	45 MIN	4	EASY

METHOD

Baking the casserole allows the ingredients to meld together, creating a hearty, satisfying dish.

CALORIES	FAT	SATURATES	PROTEIN	CARBS	SUGARS	SALT	FIBRE
400	30g	12g	25g	2g	1g	1.2g	0g

DIRECTIONS

STAGE I

1. Preheat the oven to 180°C (350°F).

2. In a skillet, cook the ground beef and bacon until browned. Drain excess fat.

STAGE II

3. In a large bowl, whisk the eggs and season with salt and pepper.

4. Combine the cooked meat and eggs in a baking dish. Top with shredded cheese if using.

5. Bake in the preheated oven for 30 minutes, or until the eggs are set.

6. Serve hot.

The casserole should be firm and golden on top. Adding cheese provides extra richness, but it can be omitted for a stricter carnivore approach.

THE
SEASONING

Season to taste.

BONE MARROW WITH SCRAMBLED EGGS

INGREDIENTS

4 BEEF MARROW BONES

4 LARGE EGGS

2 TABLESPOONS BUTTER

SALT AND PEPPER TO TASTE

METHOD
ROASTING

TIME
25 MIN

SERVING
2

DIFFICULTY
EASY

METHOD

Roasting the bone marrow and frying the eggs ensures a rich, hearty breakfast.

CALORIES	FAT	SATURATES	PROTEIN	CARBS	SUGARS	SALT	FIBRE
500	45g	20g	20g	1g	0g	1g	0g

DIRECTIONS

STAGE I

1. Preheat the oven to 200°C (400°F).

2. Place the marrow bones on a baking sheet and roast for 15-20 minutes, or until the marrow is soft and bubbly.

STAGE II

3. While the bones are roasting, heat a skillet over medium heat and add the butter.

4. Crack the eggs into the skillet and scramble until cooked to your preference. Season with salt and pepper.

5. Serve the scrambled eggs alongside the roasted bone marrow.

The bone marrow should be soft and spreadable, perfect for topping the scrambled eggs.

THE
SEASONING

Season the eggs lightly to let the rich flavour of the marrow shine.

LUNCH AND DINNER

GRILLED SALMON

INGREDIENTS

2 SALMON FILLETS (ABOUT 200 G EACH)

1 TABLESPOON OLIVE OIL

SALT AND PEPPER TO TASTE

LEMON WEDGES FOR SERVING

METHOD	TIME	SERVING	DIFFICULTY
GRILLING	20 MIN	2	EASY

METHOD

Grilling the salmon ensures a smoky flavour and crispy skin.

CALORIES	FAT	SATURATES	PROTEIN	CARBS	SUGARS	SALT	FIBRE
350	25g	5g	30g	1g	0g	0.5g	0g

DIRECTIONS

STAGE I

1. Preheat the grill to medium-high heat.
2. Rub the salmon fillets with olive oil and season with salt and pepper.

STAGE II

3. Place the salmon fillets on the grill, skin side down. Grill for 4-5 minutes on each side, or until the fish is opaque and flakes easily with a fork.
4. Serve with lemon wedges.

The salmon should have a crispy skin and a tender, flaky interior.

THE
SEASONING

Season generously for the best flavour.

ROAST DUCK

INGREDIENTS

1 WHOLE DUCK (ABOUT 2 KG)
1 ORANGE, QUARTERED
1 ONION, QUARTERED
2 CLOVES GARLIC, CRUSHED
SALT AND PEPPER TO TASTE

METHOD
ROASTING

TIME
2 HOURS

SERVING
4

DIFFICULTY
MEDIUM

METHOD
Roasting the duck ensures crispy skin and tender meat.

CALORIES	FAT	SATURATES	PROTEIN	CARBS	SUGARS	SALT	FIBRE
500	35g	10g	40g	2g	1g	1g	0g

DIRECTIONS

STAGE I

1. Preheat the oven to 180°C (350°F).

2. Pat the duck dry with paper towels. Season the cavity with salt and pepper and stuff with orange, onion, and garlic.

STAGE II

3. Place the duck on a rack in a roasting pan. Roast for 1 hour and 30 minutes to 2 hours, or until the skin is crispy and the meat is tender.

4. Let the duck rest for 10 minutes before carving.

5. Serve with the roasted vegetables from the cavity.

The roast duck should have crispy, golden skin and tender, juicy meat.

THE
SEASONING

Letting the duck rest before carving ensures the juices redistribute for a moist result.

PORK TENDERLOIN

INGREDIENTS

1 PORK TENDERLOIN (ABOUT 500G)
2 TABLESPOONS OLIVE OIL
2 CLOVES GARLIC, MINCED
1 TEASPOON ROSEMARY, CHOPPED
SALT AND PEPPER TO TASTE

METHOD	**TIME**	**SERVING**	**DIFFICULTY**
ROASTING	30 MIN	4	EASY

METHOD
Roasting the pork tenderloin ensures it is juicy and tender.

CALORIES	FAT	SATURATES	PROTEIN	CARBS	SUGARS	SALT	FIBRE
250	12g	3g	30g	1g	0g	0.8g	0g

DIRECTIONS

STAGE I

1. Preheat the oven to 200°C (400°F).
2. Rub the pork tenderloin with olive oil, garlic, rosemary, salt, and pepper.

STAGE II

3. Place the tenderloin in a roasting pan and roast for 25-30 minutes, or until the internal temperature reaches 63°C (145°F).
4. Let the pork rest for 5-10 minutes before slicing.
5. Serve immediately.

The pork tenderloin should be juicy and tender. Resting the meat before slicing ensures it remains moist.

THE
SEASONING

Season generously for the best flavour.

MEATLOAF

INGREDIENTS

500G GROUND BEEF

1 EGG

1 SMALL ONION, FINELY CHOPPED

2 CLOVES GARLIC, MINCED

50G GRATED PARMESAN CHEESE

1 TEASPOON SALT

1/2 TEASPOON BLACK PEPPER

1 TEASPOON DRIED OREGANO

METHOD	TIME	SERVING	DIFFICULTY
BAKING	1 HOUR	4	EASY

METHOD

Baking the meatloaf ensures it is cooked through and holds its shape.

CALORIES	FAT	SATURATES	PROTEIN	CARBS	SUGARS	SALT	FIBRE
350	25g	10g	30g	2g	1g	1g	0g

DIRECTIONS

STAGE I

1. Preheat the oven to 180°C (350°F).

2. In a large bowl, combine ground beef, egg, onion, garlic, Parmesan cheese, salt, black pepper, and oregano. Mix until well combined.

STAGE II

3. Shape the mixture into a loaf and place it in a baking dish.

4. Bake in the preheated oven for 50-60 minutes, or until the internal temperature reaches 70°C (160°F).

5. Let the meatloaf rest for 10 minutes before slicing.

6. Serve hot.

The meatloaf should be moist and well-seasoned. Resting the meatloaf before slicing ensures it holds its shape.

THE
SEASONING

Season to taste.

PART V

STRICT CARNIVORE (100% ANIMAL FOODS)

EMBRACING THE STRICT CARNIVORE DIET

Transitioning to the Strict Carnivore phase involves committing fully to an animal-based diet, consuming 100% of your calories from animal foods. This phase is designed for those who want to experience the ultimate benefits of the carnivore diet, focusing entirely on high-quality proteins and fats from animal sources.

UNDERSTANDING THE STRICT CARNIVORE DIET

The Strict Carnivore diet is the purest form of the carnivore lifestyle, excluding all plant-based foods. This phase emphasises consuming only animal-based products such as meat, fish, eggs, and dairy. By eliminating plant-based foods entirely, you allow your body to fully adapt to a diet that prioritises nutrient-dense animal products. This approach helps to maximise the health benefits associated with the carnivore diet, including improved mental clarity, enhanced energy levels, and better overall health.

• **Optimal Nutrient Density:** Animal-based foods are packed with essential vitamins, minerals, and amino acids that are highly bioavailable, ensuring your body gets the nutrients it needs.

• **Simplified Eating:** With a focus on a few high-quality foods, meal planning and preparation become straightforward and less time-consuming.

• **Enhanced Health:** Many people report significant improvements in health markers such as blood pressure, cholesterol levels, and inflammation.

Tips for Success:

1. **Variety in Animal Foods:** Incorporate different types of meat, fish, and organ meats to ensure a broad spectrum of nutrients.

2. **Source Quality Products:** Prioritise grass-fed, pasture-raised, and wild-caught animal products for optimal health benefits.

3. **Listen to Your Body:** Monitor how your body responds to the diet and make adjustments as needed to ensure you feel your best.

4. **Stay Hydrated:** Drink plenty of water and ensure adequate electrolyte intake to support your body's needs.

5. **Keep It Simple:** Enjoy the simplicity of the diet and focus on preparing delicious, satisfying meals with minimal ingredients.

BREAKFASTS

BEEF BACON

INGREDIENTS

---

8 SLICES OF BEEF BACON

SALT AND PEPPER TO TASTE

METHOD	TIME	SERVING	DIFFICULTY
FRYING	15 MIN	2	EASY

METHOD

Frying ensures the beef bacon becomes crispy and flavourful.

CALORIES	FAT	SATURATES	PROTEIN	CARBS	SUGARS	SALT	FIBRE
250	20g	8g	15g	0g	0g	1g	0g

DIRECTIONS

STAGE I

1. Heat a frying pan over medium heat.
2. Season the beef bacon slices with salt and pepper.

STAGE II

3. Add the bacon slices to the pan and cook until crispy, turning occasionally. This should take about 5-7 minutes.
4. Remove from the pan and drain on paper towels. Serve immediately.

Fry over medium heat to ensure even cooking and avoid burning.

THE
SEASONING

The beef bacon should be crispy and well-seasoned.

BONE BROTH BREAKFAST SOUP

INGREDIENTS

500ML BONE BROTH

2 LARGE EGGS

100G COOKED SHREDDED BEEF OR CHICKEN

SALT AND PEPPER TO TASTE

 METHOD
SIMMERING

 TIME
20 MIN

 SERVING
2

 DIFFICULTY
EASY

METHOD

Simmering the bone broth with added ingredients creates a nourishing breakfast soup.

CALORIES	FAT	SATURATES	PROTEIN	CARBS	SUGARS	SALT	FIBRE
200	12g	5g	20g	1g	0g	1g	0g

DIRECTIONS

STAGE I

1. Heat the bone broth in a pot over medium heat until it begins to simmer.

2. Crack the eggs into the simmering broth and stir gently to create ribbons of egg.

STAGE II

3. Add the cooked shredded beef or chicken to the pot and heat through.

4. Season with salt and pepper. Serve hot.

The bone broth soup should be hot and nourishing, with tender ribbons of egg and shredded meat.

THE
SEASONING

Adjust seasoning to taste for a comforting breakfast.

PORK BELLY AND EGGS

INGREDIENTS

200G PORK BELLY, SLICED

4 LARGE EGGS

SALT AND PEPPER TO TASTE

METHOD	TIME	SERVING	DIFFICULTY
FRYING	20 MIN	2	EASY

METHOD

Frying the pork belly and eggs ensures a crispy, savoury breakfast.

CALORIES	FAT	SATURATES	PROTEIN	CARBS	SUGARS	SALT	FIBRE
450	35g	15g	30g	1g	0g	1g	0g

DIRECTIONS

STAGE I

1. Heat a frying pan over medium heat.

2. Add the pork belly slices to the pan and cook until crispy, about 5-7 minutes. Remove from the pan and drain on paper towels.

STAGE II

3. In the same pan, crack the eggs and fry to your preferred doneness. Season with salt and pepper.

4. Serve the pork belly with the fried eggs.

The pork belly should be crispy, and the eggs cooked to your preference.

THE
SEASONING

Season lightly to complement the rich flavours of the pork belly.

CHICKEN LIVER PÂTÉ

INGREDIENTS

200G CHICKEN LIVERS, CLEANED

100G BEEF TALLOW OR LARD, DIVIDED

SALT TO TASTE

METHOD	TIME	SERVING	DIFFICULTY
BLENDING	30 MIN	4	MEDIUM

METHOD

Blending cooked chicken livers with butter creates a smooth, rich pâté.

CALORIES	FAT	SATURATES	PROTEIN	CARBS	SUGARS	SALT	FIBRE
300	25g	15g	15g	2g	1g	1g	0g

DIRECTIONS

STAGE I

1. Heat half of the beef tallow or lard in a frying pan over medium heat.

2. Add the chicken livers and cook until no longer pink in the centre.

STAGE II

3. Transfer the cooked livers to a blender, add the remaining beef tallow or lard, and blend until smooth. Season with salt to taste.

4. Serve chilled.

The chicken liver pâté should be smooth and creamy with a rich flavour. Ensure the livers are cooked through but not overcooked to maintain a tender texture.

THE
SEASONING

Season to taste.

LUNCH AND DINNER

GRILLED T-BONE STEAK

INGREDIENTS

2 T-BONE STEAKS (ABOUT 400G EACH)
SALT AND PEPPER TO TASTE

METHOD	TIME	SERVING	DIFFICULTY
GRILLING	20 MIN	2	EASY

METHOD

Grilling the T-bone steak ensures a smoky flavour and a perfect sear.

CALORIES	FAT	SATURATES	PROTEIN	CARBS	SUGARS	SALT	FIBRE
600	45g	15g	50g	1g	0g	1g	0g

DIRECTIONS

STAGE I

1. Preheat the grill to high heat.
2. Season steaks generously with salt and pepper.

STAGE II

3. Place the steaks on the grill and cook for 4-5 minutes on each side for medium-rare, or until they reach your desired level of doneness.
4. Let the steaks rest for a few minutes before serving.

The T-bone steaks should have a rich, smoky flavour with a perfect sear. Letting the steaks rest ensures they remain juicy and tender.

THE
SEASONING

Season generously for the best taste.

ROASTED BONE MARROW

INGREDIENTS

4 BEEF MARROW BONES
SALT AND PEPPER TO TASTE

METHOD	TIME	SERVING	DIFFICULTY
ROASTING	20 MIN	2	EASY

METHOD

Roasting the bone marrow brings out its rich, buttery flavour.

CALORIES	FAT	SATURATES	PROTEIN	CARBS	SUGARS	SALT	FIBRE
300	28g	15g	6g	0g	0g	0.5g	0g

DIRECTIONS

STAGE I

1. Preheat the oven to 220°C (425°F).

2. Place the marrow bones on a baking sheet and season with salt and pepper.

STAGE II

3. Roast in the preheated oven for 20-25 minutes, or until the marrow is soft and bubbling.

4. Serve hot.

The roasted bone marrow should be soft and spreadable.

THE
SEASONING

Season lightly to enhance the natural richness of the marrow.

LAMB SHANKS

INGREDIENTS

4 LAMB SHANKS

4 CUPS BEEF BROTH

SALT AND PEPPER TO TASTE

 METHOD
BRAISING

 **TIME**
2 HOURS
30 MIN

SERVING
4

 DIFFICULTY
MEDIUM

METHOD

Braising the lamb shanks ensures they are tender and flavourful.

CALORIES	FAT	SATURATES	PROTEIN	CARBS	SUGARS	SALT	FIBRE
600	40g	15g	50g	0g	0g	0.8g	0g

DIRECTIONS

STAGE I

1. Preheat the oven to 160°C (325°F).
2. Season the lamb shanks generously with salt.

STAGE II

3. Place the lamb shanks in a large oven-safe pot.
4. Pour in the beef bone broth, ensuring the shanks are mostly submerged.
5. Bring to a simmer on the stove, then cover and transfer to the preheated oven.
6. Braise for 2-2.5 hours, or until the lamb is tender and falling off the bone.
7. Serve hot.

The lamb shanks should be tender and falling off the bone. Braising them in beef bone broth enhances their rich flavour and keeps them moist.

THE
SEASONING

Adjust the salt to taste.

GRILLED BURGERS

INGREDIENTS

500G GROUND BEEF

1 EGG

SALT AND PEPPER TO TASTE

METHOD	TIME	SERVING	DIFFICULTY
GRILLING	20 MIN	4	EASY

METHOD

Grilling the burgers ensures they are juicy and flavourful with a smoky touch.

CALORIES	FAT	SATURATES	PROTEIN	CARBS	SUGARS	SALT	FIBRE
350	25g	10g	30g	1g	0g	0.8g	0g

DIRECTIONS

STAGE I

1. Preheat the grill to medium-high heat.
2. In a bowl, mix the ground beef with the egg, salt, and pepper. Form into four patties.

STAGE II

3. Place the patties on the grill and cook for 4-5 minutes on each side, or until they reach your desired level of doneness.
4. Serve hot.

The grilled burgers should be juicy with a smoky flavour.

THE
SEASONING

Season the meat generously and avoid overcooking to keep the burgers moist.

ROAST TURKEY

INGREDIENTS

1 WHOLE TURKEY (ABOUT 4 KG)

4 TABLESPOONS MELTED BEEF TALLOW

SALT TO TASTE

METHOD
ROASTING

TIME
3 HOURS

SERVING
8

DIFFICULTY
MEDIUM

METHOD
Roasting the turkey ensures it is juicy and tender with crispy skin.

CALORIES	FAT	SATURATES	PROTEIN	CARBS	SUGARS	SALT	FIBRE
450	25g	10g	50g	0g	0g	1g	0g

DIRECTIONS

STAGE I

1. Preheat the oven to 180°C (350°F).

2. Pat the turkey dry with paper towels. Rub the skin with melted beef tallow and season generously with salt.

STAGE II

3. Place the turkey on a rack in a roasting pan.

4. Roast in the preheated oven for 2.5 to 3 hours, or until the internal temperature reaches 75°C (165°F) and the skin is golden and crispy.

5. Let the turkey rest for 20 minutes before carving.

6. Serve hot.

The roast turkey should have crispy skin and juicy, tender meat. Letting the turkey rest before carving ensures the juices redistribute for a moist result.

THE
SEASONING

Season generously with salt for the best flavour.

THANK YOU FOR CHOOSING **"THE CARNIVORE TRANSITION DIET COOKBOOK FOR BEGINNERS 2024."**

I HOPE THIS BOOK HAS PROVIDED YOU WITH VALUABLE INSIGHTS, DELICIOUS RECIPES, AND A COMPREHENSIVE GUIDE TO EMBARKING ON YOUR CARNIVORE JOURNEY. YOUR DEDICATION TO IMPROVING YOUR HEALTH AND WELL-BEING THROUGH A CARNIVORE DIET IS COMMENDABLE, AND I AM HONOURED TO BE A PART OF YOUR JOURNEY.

I WOULD LOVE TO HEAR ABOUT YOUR EXPERIENCES WITH THIS COOKBOOK. YOUR FEEDBACK IS INCREDIBLY IMPORTANT TO ME AND HELPS ME TO CONTINUALLY IMPROVE MY OFFERINGS. IF YOU HAVE ENJOYED THE RECIPES AND FOUND THE INFORMATION HELPFUL, PLEASE CONSIDER LEAVING A REVIEW.

THANK YOU AGAIN FOR YOUR SUPPORT, AND WE WISH YOU GREAT SUCCESS AND HEALTH ON YOUR CARNIVORE JOURNEY!

SINCERELY,

Kimberly Stephens